CHILDREN'S PROGRAM BUILDER

No. 11

LILLENAS® DRAMA

CHILDREN'S PROGRAM BUILDER No. 11

Creative Resources for Program Directors

Compiled by Kim Messer

lillenas PUBLISHING COMPANY | PO Box 419527 Kansas City, MO 64141

Questions? Please write or call:
Lillenas Publishing Company
Drama Resources
P.O. Box 419527
Kansas City, MO 64141
Phone: 816-931-1900 • Fax: 816-412-8390
E-mail: drama@lillenas.com
Web Site: www.lillenasdrama.com

Cover design: Doug Bennett
Executive Editor: Kim Messer
Copy Editor: Kimberly Meiste
Manuscript Formatting: Karen Phillips

Table of Contents

Graded Recitations

Worship Builders

PRESCHOOL RECITATIONS

Proud of My Church

I'm proud of my church
And glad I am here
To help celebrate
Its [50th] year.

Margaret Primrose

Time to Give Thanks

It's time to thank God
For each parent and friend,
For our food, home, and clothes,
And for life without end.

Margaret Primrose

A Little Sheep

A little sheep so cute and sweet
Lay down beside the shepherd's
feet.
A little sheep so young and pure
Slept peacefully and did not stir.

Wanda E. Brunstetter

We're Thankful

ALL: Dear God,
CHILD 1 *(displaying open Bible):*
We're thankful for the
Bible
That others help us read.
CHILD 2 *(displaying flower seed
packet):*
Plant its words in our
hearts
Like many little seeds.
CHILD 3 *(holding watering can):*
Water the seeds with
love,
Helping them to grow,
CHILD 4 *(holding basket of fruit):*
So we may bear good
fruit
Everywhere we go.
ALL: Amen!

Nancy Merical

RECITATIONS AGES 5 TO 7

Thanks!

CHILD 1: It takes a lot of practice
To sing for you and me,
To make the organ thunder,
Then whisper quietly.

CHILD 2: But music is important
Each time we meet to pray,
So say a great big thank you
To those who sing and play.

(After the piece all the children lead a round of applause for the musicians.)

Margaret Primrose

Making God Smile

CHILD 1: Anyone can pick up trash
Or put a book in place.
Anyone can say a prayer
And hum "Amazing Grace."

CHILD 2: But when we join together
In worship, work, and play,
I think it makes God happy
And brightens all His day.

Margaret Primrose

I Thank Him

CHILD 1: I thank God for the
mountains.
I thank Him for the skies.
I thank Him for the
mighty acts
That all around me lie.

CHILD 2: I thank God for His
kindness,
I thank Him for His love.
I thank Him for His only
Son
That came from heav'n
above.

CHILD 3: I thank God for His
goodness.
I thank Him every day.
I thank Him for His
faithfulness
That keeps me lest I stray.

CHILD 4: I thank God for His
patience.
Each day I praise Him
more.
I thank Him for His holy
Word
That forever will endure.

CHILD 5: I thank God for the
flowers.
I thank Him for each tree.
I thank Him for His
loving Son
That died to make me
free.

CHILD 6: I thank God for His
power
And great, strong, loving
care.
I thank Him for the day
That I will meet Him in
the air!

Mary Wisham Fenstermacher

RECITATIONS AGES 8 TO 10

God Bless Our Church

Dear Jesus, bless our church,
The choir, and all the people.
And thank You for the pews,
The doors, the lights, the steeple.

The windows, walls, and roof,
The carpet, halls, and stairs,
And don't forget to bless
All the kindergarten chairs.
Amen.

Margaret Primrose

A Prayer of Thanksgiving

CHILD 1: We thank You, Heavenly Father, for blessings from above.
We thank You for Your kindness shown to us in love.

CHILD 2: We thank You for Your Son, the Savior of us all.
We thank You for forgiveness on Him whose name we call.

CHILD 3: We thank You, Heavenly Father, for Your sustaining grace.
We thank You for the power to win the human race.

CHILD 4: We thank You for Heaven, our home beyond the skies.
We thank You for the safety of Your ever watchful eyes.

Wanda E. Brunstetter

Evangelism / Missions

RECITATION AGES 5 TO 7

Go . . . Tell

Some women came with spices
For One no longer dead.
An angel met them at the tomb
And this is what he said:
"Go . . . tell His disciples."

Afraid, yet filled with wonder,
They ran to spread the word.
The risen Savior met them
And this is what they heard:
"Go . . . tell My brothers."

Christ came as they were gathered
On the slopes of Galilee
And gave to them a message
That extends to you and me:
"Go . . . tell the world."

Margaret Primrose

Sunday School

RECITATION AGES 5 TO 7

Sunday School's Great

(Other names may be used)

Katie says, "It's awesome,"
And Megan says, "It's cool."
But I just say, "It's great
To be in Sunday School."

Margaret Primrose

Teacher Appreciation

PRESCHOOL RECITATION

My Teacher

(Follow this short verse with a song.)

My teacher's always ready
If the weather's bright or gray.
I'm glad that she loves Jesus
And helps us sing and pray.

Margaret Primrose

RECITATIONS AGES 5 TO 7

Special

I picked a pretty flower
To bring to class today,
But on the way I broke it
And threw the stem away.

I crushed the pretty flower
In the pocket of my coat.
My teacher liked it anyway
And said that it would float.

She put it on the table.
It's in a special vase.
She says I'm like that flower—
I have a special place.

She told me Jesus loves me
No matter what I do.
There's something else I'm
learning—
My teacher's special too.

Margaret Primrose

Our Hearts Are with You

(Several boys and girls come on stage or to the front of the classroom, each holding a different "heart" designed with colorful paper, lace, and flower decorations. At the end of the recitation, they could hand out the "hearts" to the teachers.)

CHILD 1: Here is my "heart" I give
to you
With many thoughts and
feelings true.
CHILD 2: Our teachers help us
learn and grow.
So on Valentine's Day we
wish to show
CHILD 3: Our love and respect with
these designs.
Won't you be our year-
round Valentines?

Jean Conder Soule

Thank You, Teacher

I thought we paid our teacher
From what we children bring.
But it buys books and pencils—
She doesn't get a thing.

A smile is little payment
For all she has to do.
So now with your permission,
I think I'll hug her too.

Margaret Primrose

Pastor's Appreciation

PRESCHOOL RECITATION

We Love Our Pastor

(Recited by a group of children.)

We love our pastor
And just want to say
We're glad that you're here
And want you to stay.

Margaret Primrose

RECITATIONS AGES 5 TO 7

Where Does Pastor Work?

CHILD: Mom, where does Pastor work?
I see him in his car.
Does he spend all his time
Just riding near and far?

I know he picks up trash
That we throw on the floor,
And yesterday I saw him
At Mr. Rogers' door.

MOTHER: Make no mistake, my child,
Our pastor doesn't shirk.
Taking care of people
Is lots and lots of work.

He studies, prays, and writes
Sometimes till late at night,
So he can preach his best
And help us do what's right.

Margaret Primrose

Thanks, Pastor

CHILD 1: Our pastor took some kids to camp
Before the sun was bright,
Although he didn't get much sleep—
The phone rang half the night.

CHILD 2: He does lots more than preach and pray,
Lock doors, and drive the van.
He fills out forms and dusts the pews,
Has dinner when he can,

CHILD 3: Then goes on errands far and near
In weather foul or fair
To help the poor and cheer the sick,
And if they die, he's there.

CHILD 4: His life's not always full of fun,
So if you're glad that God
Sent him to be our special friend,
Please stand and applaud.

(Leads congregation in applause)

Margaret Primrose

Thanksgiving

PRESCHOOL RECITATION

Our First Thanksgiving

(A recitation for eight children: 4 wearing Pilgrim hats, and 4 wearing Indian head feathers.)

INDIAN 1: Our first Thanksgiving
was a wonderful day.

PILGRIM 1: We ate together and
took time to pray.

INDIAN 2: We shared from our
gardens the bounty we
had,

PILGRIM 2: And giving much
thanks, our hearts were
glad.

INDIAN 3: Corn and other
vegetables were what
we ate,

PILGRIM 3: On that very historic
and memorable day.

INDIAN 4: Wild turkeys and deer
meat were eaten too,

PILGRIM 4: God had blessed us
richly—that we knew!

Wanda E. Brunstetter

RECITATIONS AGES 5 TO 7

Thanksgiving Day

CHILD 1: Dear God, pilgrims were thankful, and I am too,
For the freedom we have to worship You.

CHILD 2: I'm thankful for my parents who help me each day
To learn about Jesus and teach me to pray.

CHILD 3: I'm thankful for my teacher in Sunday School
Who teaches me to live by Your Golden Rule.

CHILD 4: I'm thankful for friends so loving and caring
Who teach me all about giving and sharing.

CHILD 5: God, you give us so much that I'd like to say,
"Why don't we make every day
Thanksgiving Day?"

Nancy Merical

A Thanksgiving Tribute

(Each CHILD *holds up a letter which spells the word "Thanksgiving")*

ALL: For the following we are thankful—

CHILD 1: **T** — is for Triune—a great God, three in one.

CHILD 2: **H** — is for Heaven, the place where all Christians someday go.

CHILD 3: **A** — is for Abundance, the love of Christ excels.

CHILD 4: **N** — is for Neighbor, for whom we should do only good.

CHILD 5: **K** — is for our King, our Lord and God.

CHILD 6: **S** — is for the Son of God, the sacrificial Lamb.

CHILD 7: **G** — is for God's love, available to all.

CHILD 8: **I** — is for Inheritance, which each believer has.

CHILD 9: **V** — is for Victory we find through faith in Christ.

CHILD 10: **I** — is for Intercession, the Holy Spirit makes.

CHILD 11: **N** — is for the Nail prints, placed in our Savior's hands.

CHILD 12: **G** — is for the Gift of life, which can only come from God.

Wanda E. Brunstetter

RECITATIONS AGES 8 TO 10

Thanksgiving Plans

We've turkey and potatoes,
Green beans, hot rolls, and pie,
And Grandma brought some
salad—
Our plates are piled up high.

But down the street from our
home,
A house about to fall
Has six or seven children
And little food at all.

My mother's getting ready
To take some food their way
And make the family happy
On this Thanksgiving Day.

I'm glad that Jesus taught us
What joy it is to give.
We'll tell them that He loves them
And died that they may live.

Margaret Primrose

Counting My Blessings

God sends so many blessings—
To count them, there's no way.
I'll list a few from A to Z
On this Thanksgiving Day.

I thank the Lord for apples,
For Bibles, candy, drapes,
For elephants and flowers—
I'm also fond of grapes.

I'm thankful, too, for horses,
For Jesus, ice, and keys,
For lamps and mugs and nurses,
For onions and for peas.

It's fun to hear a duck's quack
And watch a rabbit hop.
The sun is also pleasant.
I like to spin my top.

A ukulele's notes are sweet.
I'm thankful for our van.
I'm also glad that Daddy
Found good work for a man.

It's good that there are X-rays;
I'm thankful you are you;
And though the Z's a hard one,
I really like the zoo.

Now why not make your own list?
It doesn't have to rhyme.
Then keep on adding to it
Whenever you have time.

Margaret Primrose

Thanksgiving Thoughts

(This can be done as a choral poem with speakers in Pilgrim costumes. A small ship resembling the famous Mayflower can be constructed from cardboard, painted, and "sailed" into the classroom or across the stage at the beginning by younger children as the older children read.)

We thank You, Lord, for giving us
A wonderful place to be
Where Pilgrims came aboard a ship
Across a stormy sea.

They landed their ship at Plymouth Rock
And established a home, we know.
The friendly Indians welcomed them
And taught them the crops to grow.

Because of their trials that winter time
They decided to set aside
A special day to thank the Lord
For the blessings He supplied.

Now still today we have a feast,
November's celebration
To remember those hard-working folk
Who helped to found our nation.

So, as we enjoy turkey treats
And all those desserts so grand,
Let us not forget our Pilgrim friends
Who worshipped God in this land.

It's because of them we live in peace
In a country large and free.
Let us bow our heads and say a prayer
And be grateful, both you and me!

Jean Conder Soule

Readings & Programs

Jesus Is the Answer

by C. R. Scheidies

(Can be done with three individuals or three groups; or two individuals and one young group for CHORUS. *Have* CHORUS *group at CS between the other children.)*

OLDER CHILD 1: As I travel down life's road,
And find it with boulders filled,
I clasp the hand of Jesus,
He who bid the waves be still.

CHORUS: Jesus is the answer.
Jesus is the way.
I know He is with me
Each and every day.

OLDER CHILD 2: Jesus came as an infant
In a lonely stable bed,
Heralded by heavenly angels.
The news by lowly shepherds spread.

CHORUS: Jesus is the answer.
Jesus is the way.
I know He is with me
Each and every day.

OLDER CHILD 1: Jesus raised in obscurity
Exploded on the scene.
His compassion as His miracles
Confounded the Pharisees.

CHORUS: Jesus is the answer.
Jesus is the way.
I know He is with me
Each and every day.

OLDER CHILD 2: He lived a life of love and truth
In order that He

Might take upon himself the cross,
To die for you and me.

CHORUS: Jesus is the answer.
Jesus is the way.
I know He is with me
Each and every day.

OLDER CHILD 1: Even the grave could not
Hold God's only Son,

OLDER CHILD 2: Raised in glory, our Savior King
His earthly mission done.

ALL: Yes, Jesus is the answer.
He's the only way.
Now I give my life to Him
On this very day.
Amen!

Back to School

by Faye Nyce

PASTOR:

It's late August,
Soon our children will be heading back to school,
Leaving the home either day by day,
Or for a semester; perhaps even an entire school year.
What are our reflections as we consider
The implications of this separation?
Is it a relief to have them out of the house?
Will it feel good to have a quieter home? The phone back again?
Or do we wish to hold on to them?
Do we have a healthy attitude about this separation?

TEACHER OF ELEMENTARY-AGE CHILDREN:

It's late August—the summer has passed with tremendous speed!
How can I be ready to go back to the schoolroom?
Back to twenty-eight energetic children,
Each with his/her own needs, abilities, and disabilities.
Some coming from painful experiences at home,
Others from homes with every advantage.
All with so much potential for trouble or success.
Lord, I will need wisdom from You—and patience, too.
Give me the creativity that allows me to make this a good year
For each child.

PARENTS OF ELEMENTARY-AGE CHILDREN:

It's late August—nearly time for school to start again!
As we buy new school clothes, I'm both glad and sad.
Glad that my children have an opportunity to learn,
Sad as I reflect on possible undesirable influences.
A bit distressed that the children are another year older,
And there are fewer years left for them with us.
I'm anxious about entrusting them into the supervision
Of a teacher I do not know.
Lord, give due portion of love and care to each of us for the good
Of each child.

ELEMENTARY-AGE CHILD:

It's late August—summer went so fast!
I'm not really ready to sit at a desk all day,
To write reports and memorize more math.
I liked the lazy days of the past few months
And the family trip to the mountains.
Yet, I'm anxious to see my friends
And catch up on what they did all summer.
But, dear God, I'm just a little scared about fitting in
With all the other kids again.
Please, God, put Your arms around me and keep me close.

PARENTS OF COLLEGE-AGE SON OR DAUGHTER:

It's late August—Where have the years gone?
Our child is ready for college.
How far away this day seemed when
We birthed this one.
Those years of diapers and playing on the beach
Are gone, not to return.
We have done our part in raising this young one.
Now we will hand him/her over into God's care
As he/she walks on into the unknown.
You are with him/her to guide him/her, Lord, when we no longer can.

COLLEGE STUDENT:

Ah, at last I will taste freedom.
Going away from home—from Mom and Dad.
To be my own boss, make my own decisions
With no one breathing down my neck.
Nevertheless, I'm determined to do what is right.
I want to walk in Christ's way, but in my own style;
To attempt to live Christ-like with my own flair;
To choose my friends carefully, but
Without the appraisal of my parents.
Lord, you know I love and respect them;
I'm just ready to fly from the nest.

PASTOR:

As we send our sons and daughters off to school
Whether it be first time to preschool,
Or all the way through to college,
We commit them into Your care.
We know You love them even more than we love them.
Yet our humanness can hardly let loose.
We are thankful that You are everywhere
And we will continue to pray for them daily.
We believe You will protect our sons and daughters
Wherever they are.

Children's Day Choral Reading

by Faye Nyce

LEADER: "Hear, O Israel: The LORD our God, the LORD is one. Love the LORD your God with all your heart and with all your soul and with all your strength. These commandments that I give you today are to be upon your hearts. Impress them on your children. Talk about them when you sit at home and when you walk along the road, when you lie down and when you get up. Tie them as symbols on your hands and bind them on your foreheads. Write them on the doorframes of your houses and on your gates." (Deut. 6:4-9)

PEOPLE: It is our desire to be faithful in teaching the next generation about our loving and wise God.

CHILD 1: Here we are—with open minds, eager to learn.

LEADER: Our children are our dearest treasure. They are children of blessing and hope.

PEOPLE: The church is people—big people and little people—all in God's care.

CHILD 2: I am important. God made me.

LEADER: Joel 1:3 says, "Tell it to your children, and let your children tell it to their children, and their children to the next generation."

PEOPLE: This is our goal—that the message of God's love not be lost from neglect or default.

CHILD 3: Teach us the stories of the Bible. Teach us to sing the songs that you have known.

LEADER: Jesus said, "Let the little children come to me, and do not hinder them, for the kingdom of heaven belongs to such as these . . . he had placed his hands on them . . ." (Matt. 19:14, 15)

PEOPLE: We dedicate ourselves to instructing and guiding the children among us in the way of the One who loved us and gave His life for us.

CHILD 4: We want to learn from you. We are following in your footsteps.

LEADER: Let us pray—Our kind and loving Heavenly Father, we thank You for the blessing of the children. They are Yours, but You have loaned them to us for this short time. As we teach and guide them, we plead for wisdom and patience. Give us what we need so that we will be consistent in word and deed. We aim to be good examples for their journey of life. We pray in Jesus' name. Amen.